Rebuilding America: A Path to Renewal

Charting a Course Towards a Brighter Future

James E. Davidson II

Table of Contents

- Reflecting on Progress Made

- Ensuring Long-Term Sustainability

- Adaptability and Resilience

- Continued Innovation and Growth

- Looking Towards the Future

- Conclusion

Chapter 1

Understanding the Foundations

Introduction:

America, once a beacon of freedom, democracy, and opportunity, has faced numerous challenges that have eroded its standing in the world. To restore America to its former glory, it's imperative to understand the foundational principles upon which it was built and how they have been tested over time. This chapter will delve into the core values that define America and explore how they can guide us in rebuilding a stronger and more resilient nation.

The Founding Principles:

At its core, America was founded on the principles of liberty, democracy, and equality. The Declaration of

Independence famously proclaims that all men are created equal and endowed with certain unalienable rights, including life, liberty, and the pursuit of happiness. These principles formed the basis of the American experiment and inspired generations of people around the world.

Liberty:

Liberty lies at the heart of the American identity. It is the freedom to think, speak, and act without undue restraint from government or other individuals. However, throughout history, America has grappled with defining the boundaries of liberty, particularly in times of national crisis. From the Alien and Sedition Acts of the 18th century to the Patriot Act in the wake of 9/11, there have been moments when civil liberties have been curtailed in the name of national security.

To restore America to its former glory, we must reaffirm our commitment to liberty while also recognizing the need for balance and nuance in protecting national security. This means upholding constitutional rights, such as freedom of speech, religion, and assembly, while also ensuring that necessary measures are in place to safeguard the safety and security of all citizens.

Democracy:

America's founders envisioned a government of the people, by the people, and for the people. Democracy is the cornerstone of American governance, providing citizens with the opportunity to participate in the decision-making process through free and fair elections. However, the integrity of America's democratic institutions has come under scrutiny in recent years, with concerns about voter suppression, gerrymandering, and the influence of money in politics.

To restore faith in American democracy, we must take decisive action to strengthen electoral integrity, expand access to voting, and reduce the influence of special interests. This may involve implementing reforms such as automatic voter registration, independent redistricting commissions, and campaign finance reform. By empowering citizens to fully participate in the democratic process, we can ensure that government remains accountable to the people it serves.

Equality:

America has long struggled to live up to its promise of equality for all. From the institution of slavery to the fight for civil rights, the journey towards equality has been marked by both progress and setbacks. While significant strides have been made in expanding civil rights and opportunities for marginalized communities, systemic inequalities persist in areas such as education, employment, and criminal justice.

To restore America to its former glory, we must confront these inequalities head-on and work towards creating a more just and equitable society. This may involve policies such as affirmative action, criminal justice reform, and investments in underserved communities. Additionally, we must foster a culture of inclusion and empathy, where all individuals are treated with dignity and respect regardless of their race, gender, or background.

Challenges to the Founding Principles:

Despite the lofty ideals upon which America was founded, there have been numerous challenges that have tested the resilience of its founding principles. From the Civil War to the Civil Rights Movement, America has faced moments of internal strife and division that threatened to tear the nation apart. Today, we continue to grapple with issues such as polarization, inequality, and social unrest that undermine the fabric of our society.

To restore America to its former glory, we must confront these challenges with courage and conviction. This will require a renewed commitment to dialogue, compromise, and mutual understanding across ideological divides. By bridging our differences and working together towards common goals, we can forge a stronger and more united nation that honors the legacy of those who came before us.

Conclusion:

Restoring America to its former glory will require a deep understanding of the foundational principles upon which it was built and a steadfast commitment to upholding them in the face of adversity. By embracing liberty, democracy, and equality as guiding values, we can chart a course towards a brighter future for all Americans. It will not be easy, but with determination and resolve, we can reclaim the promise of America and build a nation that is truly worthy of admiration and respect.

Chapter 2

Economic Revitalization

Introduction:

Economic prosperity is essential for the well-being of a nation and its citizens. In recent years, America has faced economic challenges ranging from stagnant wages and rising inequality to declining infrastructure and a changing job market. However, by implementing strategic policies and investing in key areas, we can revitalize the economy and create opportunities for all Americans.

Assessing the Economic Landscape:

Before diving into specific strategies for economic revitalization, it's crucial to understand the current state of the economy. Despite periods of growth, many Americans continue to struggle financially. Wages have stagnated for decades, while the cost of living has risen, leaving millions of families feeling economically insecure. Furthermore, globalization and technological advancements have transformed the job market, leading to job displacement and wage polarization.

In addition to these domestic challenges, America faces global economic competition and geopolitical uncertainties that impact trade, investment, and economic growth. Addressing these multifaceted issues requires a comprehensive approach that tackles both domestic and international economic challenges.

Strategies for Growth:

To kickstart economic revitalization, we must prioritize strategic investments in key areas that drive long-term growth and prosperity. These investments should focus on infrastructure, education, and innovation, laying the foundation for a stronger and more competitive economy.

Investment in Infrastructure:

America's infrastructure is in dire need of modernization and repair. Our roads, bridges, ports, and airports are outdated and crumbling, hindering economic productivity and growth. By investing in infrastructure projects, we can create jobs, improve connectivity, and boost economic activity.

A robust infrastructure plan should include investments in transportation, energy, water systems, and broadband access. These investments not only create immediate job opportunities but also lay the groundwork for sustained economic growth by enhancing productivity and efficiency across various sectors of the economy.

Education Reform:

Investing in education is critical for building a skilled workforce and ensuring future economic competitiveness. However, America's education system faces numerous challenges, including inadequate funding, inequitable access, and outdated curricula.

To revitalize education, we must prioritize reforms that improve access to quality education for all students, regardless of their background or zip code. This includes increasing funding for public schools, expanding access to early childhood education, and supporting teachers with professional development and resources.

In addition to traditional K-12 education, we must also invest in post-secondary education and vocational training to equip workers with the skills they need to succeed in today's economy. This includes expanding access to affordable higher education and promoting apprenticeship programs and vocational training opportunities.

Innovation and Entrepreneurship:

Innovation is the lifeblood of a dynamic economy, driving productivity gains, creating new industries, and fostering job creation. To stimulate innovation and entrepreneurship, we must create an environment that encourages risk-taking, experimentation, and investment in research and development.

Government can play a critical role in supporting innovation through policies that promote research funding, intellectual property rights, and technology transfer. Additionally, we must invest in entrepreneurship education and support programs that provide aspiring entrepreneurs with the resources and mentorship they need to turn their ideas into successful businesses.

Addressing Income Inequality:

While economic growth is essential, it must be inclusive to truly benefit all Americans. Addressing income inequality is not only a matter of fairness but also essential for sustaining long-term economic growth. When wealth and opportunity are concentrated in the hands of a few, it stifles consumer demand, undermines social cohesion, and hinders upward mobility.

To address income inequality, we must pursue policies that promote fair wages, strengthen social safety nets, and ensure that everyone has access to opportunities for economic advancement. This may include raising the minimum wage, expanding access to affordable housing and healthcare, and implementing progressive taxation policies.

Conclusion:

Economic revitalization is essential for restoring America to its former glory and ensuring prosperity for all Americans. By investing in infrastructure, education, and innovation, and addressing income inequality, we can lay the groundwork for a stronger, more resilient economy that creates opportunities for all. However, achieving economic revitalization will require political will, bipartisan cooperation, and a long-term commitment to investing in America's future.

Chapter 3

Education Reform

Introduction:

Education is the cornerstone of a thriving society, providing individuals with the knowledge, skills, and opportunities they need to succeed. However, America's education system is facing significant challenges that threaten to undermine its ability to prepare students for the demands of the 21st century. In this chapter, we will explore the current state of education in America and propose reforms to improve access to quality education for all students.

The State of Education in America:

America's education system is often hailed as the bedrock of its success, but it is also a system in crisis.

Despite significant investments in education over the years, outcomes remain uneven, with stark disparities along racial, socioeconomic, and geographic lines. Too many students, particularly those from low-income and minority backgrounds, are falling behind and failing to reach their full potential.

One of the biggest challenges facing America's education system is inequitable access to resources and opportunities. Schools in low-income communities often lack adequate funding, experienced teachers, and essential resources, leading to lower academic achievement and higher dropout rates. Furthermore, disparities in access to early childhood education, advanced coursework, and extracurricular activities perpetuate inequalities from an early age.

Improving Access and Quality:

To address these disparities and improve outcomes for all students, we must prioritize reforms that expand access to quality education and ensure that every child has the opportunity to succeed. This includes investments in early childhood education, K-12 schools, and post-secondary education, as well as initiatives to support teachers and improve school environments.

STEM Education:

In today's increasingly technological and globalized world, STEM (science, technology, engineering, and mathematics) education is more important than ever. Yet, many American students lack access to high-quality STEM education opportunities, particularly in underserved communities. By investing in STEM education, we can prepare students for the jobs of the future and ensure that America remains competitive in the global economy.

This may include initiatives to expand access to STEM coursework, support STEM teachers with professional development and resources, and promote hands-on learning experiences through partnerships with industry and community organizations. Additionally, efforts to increase diversity and representation in STEM fields are essential for ensuring that all students have the opportunity to pursue careers in these high-demand fields.

Vocational Training:

Not all students are best served by a traditional four-year college education. For many students, vocational training and apprenticeship programs offer a viable pathway to success. However, vocational education programs have been historically underfunded and undervalued in America, leading to a shortage of skilled workers in key industries.

To address this gap, we must invest in vocational training programs that provide students with the skills and credentials they need to succeed in the workforce. This includes expanding access to apprenticeship programs, partnering with employers to develop industry-specific training programs, and providing financial incentives for students to pursue vocational education.

The Role of Teachers and Schools:

At the heart of any education system are its teachers and schools. Teachers play a crucial role in shaping the minds and futures of their students, yet many teachers face significant challenges, including low salaries, inadequate resources, and lack of support. Additionally, schools themselves often grapple with issues such as overcrowding, outdated facilities, and safety concerns.

To support teachers and schools, we must invest in recruiting and retaining high-quality educators, providing them with the training, resources, and support they need to succeed. This may include initiatives to raise teacher salaries, reduce class sizes, and modernize school facilities. Additionally, efforts to promote school safety and create supportive and inclusive school environments are essential for fostering student success.

Conclusion:

Education reform is essential for ensuring that all students have access to the knowledge, skills, and opportunities they need to succeed in the 21st century. By investing in STEM education, vocational training, and supporting teachers and schools, we can create a more equitable and inclusive education system that prepares students for the challenges and opportunities of the future. However, achieving meaningful education reform will require political will, community engagement, and a long-term commitment to investing in America's most valuable resource—its children.

Chapter 4

Healthcare Overhaul

Introduction:

Access to affordable and quality healthcare is a fundamental human right and a cornerstone of a thriving society. However, America's healthcare system is plagued by inefficiencies, inequities, and skyrocketing costs that leave millions of Americans uninsured or underinsured. In this chapter, we will explore the current state of healthcare in America and propose comprehensive reforms to ensure access to healthcare for all citizens.

Assessing the Healthcare System:

America's healthcare system is a complex web of public and private insurers, healthcare providers, pharmaceutical companies, and government agencies. While advances in medical technology and innovation have improved patient outcomes, the system itself is characterized by fragmentation, inefficiency, and inequity.

One of the biggest challenges facing America's healthcare system is access. Despite the passage of the Affordable Care Act (ACA) in 2010, millions of Americans remain uninsured, unable to afford coverage or ineligible for public programs. Additionally, even those with insurance face barriers to accessing care, including high deductibles, copayments, and out-of-pocket expenses.

Another major issue is cost. Healthcare spending in the United States far exceeds that of other developed countries, yet outcomes are often worse. The high cost of healthcare puts a strain on individuals, families, businesses, and government budgets, leading to financial hardship and medical debt for many Americans.

Ensuring Access and Affordability:

To address these challenges and create a healthcare system that works for all Americans, we must pursue comprehensive reforms that prioritize access, affordability, and quality of care. This includes ensuring that every American has access to comprehensive health coverage, regardless of their income, employment status, or pre-existing conditions.

Universal Healthcare:

One potential solution to America's healthcare woes is the adoption of a universal healthcare system, where healthcare coverage is guaranteed to all citizens as a right of citizenship. Under a universal healthcare system, the government acts as a single payer, negotiating prices with healthcare providers and covering the cost of care through taxes.

There are several models of universal healthcare, including single-payer systems like those found in Canada and the United Kingdom, as well as multi-payer systems with universal coverage like those found in Germany and Switzerland. While the specifics may vary, the overarching goal is to ensure that everyone has access to necessary medical care without facing financial hardship.

Preventative Care:

In addition to expanding access to healthcare coverage, we must also prioritize preventative care and public health initiatives to keep Americans healthy and reduce the burden of chronic disease. Preventative care, including vaccinations, screenings, and lifestyle interventions, can help identify and address health issues early, before they become more serious and costly to treat.

By investing in preventative care and public health initiatives, we can reduce healthcare costs, improve patient outcomes, and promote overall well-being. This may include initiatives to promote healthy behaviors, improve access to nutritious foods and safe environments, and address social determinants of health such as poverty, housing instability, and food insecurity.

Embracing Technology and Innovation:

Technology has the potential to revolutionize healthcare delivery, making it more efficient, accessible, and patient-centered. From telemedicine and remote monitoring to electronic health records and artificial intelligence, digital technologies offer new opportunities to improve healthcare outcomes and experiences for patients and providers alike.

By embracing technology and innovation, we can streamline administrative processes, improve care coordination, and empower patients to take a more active role in managing their health. Additionally, digital health tools can help address healthcare disparities by expanding access to care in underserved communities and improving communication between patients and providers.

Conclusion:

Overhauling America's healthcare system is a complex and daunting task, but it is one that is necessary to ensure that all Americans have access to affordable and quality healthcare. By pursuing comprehensive reforms that prioritize access, affordability, and quality of care, we can create a healthcare system that works for all Americans, regardless of their income, employment status, or health needs. However, achieving meaningful healthcare reform will require political will, bipartisan cooperation, and a commitment to putting the needs of patients first.

Chapter 5

Infrastructure Renewal

Introduction:

Infrastructure is the backbone of a modern society, providing essential services and facilitating economic activity. From roads and bridges to public transportation and broadband networks, infrastructure plays a critical role in connecting communities, facilitating commerce, and ensuring public safety. However, America's infrastructure is in dire need of renewal and investment to address decades of neglect and decay. In this chapter, we will explore the state of America's infrastructure and propose strategies for modernization and renewal.

The Need for Modernization:

America's infrastructure is aging and crumbling, with many roads, bridges, and other critical assets in need of repair or replacement. Decades of underinvestment, deferred maintenance, and population growth have taken their toll, leading to congestion, delays, and safety hazards across the country.

According to the American Society of Civil Engineers (ASCE), America's infrastructure received a dismal grade of "C-" in its most recent report card, with key sectors such as roads, bridges, and transit earning even lower grades. The ASCE estimates that the United States needs to invest trillions of dollars over the next decade to bring its infrastructure up to a state of good repair and ensure its long-term sustainability.

Investing in Infrastructure:

To address America's infrastructure challenges, we must prioritize strategic investments in key sectors such as transportation, energy, water, and broadband. These investments will not only create jobs and stimulate economic growth but also improve quality of life, enhance productivity, and promote environmental sustainability.

Roads and Bridges:

America's roads and bridges are in desperate need of repair and modernization. Many roads are riddled with potholes, congestion is rampant, and bridges are structurally deficient or functionally obsolete. By investing in road and bridge repair and expansion projects, we can improve safety, reduce congestion, and enhance connectivity between communities.

Public Transportation:

Public transportation plays a vital role in providing mobility options for millions of Americans, particularly in urban areas. However, many transit systems suffer from aging infrastructure, inadequate funding, and declining ridership. By investing in public transportation infrastructure, we can improve service reliability, expand access to jobs and opportunities, and reduce greenhouse gas emissions.

Broadband Access:

In today's digital age, access to high-speed internet is no longer a luxury but a necessity. Yet, millions of Americans lack access to reliable broadband service, particularly in rural and underserved areas. By investing in broadband infrastructure, we can bridge the digital divide, expand access to educational and economic opportunities, and promote economic development in communities across the country.

Sustainability and Climate Resilience:

As we invest in infrastructure renewal, we must also prioritize sustainability and climate resilience to mitigate the impacts of climate change and ensure the long-term viability of our infrastructure systems. This includes incorporating green infrastructure practices, such as permeable pavements and green roofs, to manage stormwater and reduce flooding. Additionally, investing in renewable energy and energy-efficient technologies can help reduce greenhouse gas emissions and promote environmental sustainability.

Conclusion:

Infrastructure renewal is essential for ensuring the continued prosperity and well-being of America's communities. By investing in roads, bridges, public transportation, broadband, and other critical infrastructure assets, we can create jobs, stimulate economic growth, and improve quality of life for all Americans. However, achieving meaningful infrastructure renewal will require political will, bipartisan cooperation, and a commitment to investing in America's future. With strategic investments and a long-term vision, we can build a stronger, more resilient infrastructure that meets the needs of future generations.

Chapter 6

Energy Independence

Introduction:

Energy is the lifeblood of modern society, powering our homes, businesses, and transportation systems. However, America's dependence on fossil fuels poses significant challenges, including environmental degradation, geopolitical instability, and economic vulnerability to price fluctuations. In this chapter, we will explore strategies for transitioning to renewable energy sources and reducing America's reliance on fossil fuels.

The Case for Renewable Energy:

Renewable energy sources, such as solar, wind, and hydroelectric power, offer numerous benefits over fossil fuels. Unlike finite fossil fuel reserves, renewable energy sources are abundant, sustainable, and environmentally friendly. Additionally, renewable energy technologies have become increasingly cost-competitive in recent years, making them an attractive option for meeting America's energy needs.

Transitioning to Renewable Energy:

To transition to renewable energy, we must invest in infrastructure, innovation, and policy reforms that support the deployment and adoption of renewable energy technologies. This includes expanding renewable energy generation capacity, modernizing the electrical grid, and promoting energy efficiency and conservation efforts.

Solar Power:

Solar power has emerged as one of the fastest-growing sources of renewable energy in the United States. Solar panels convert sunlight into electricity, providing a clean and abundant source of power for homes, businesses, and utilities. By investing in solar power infrastructure and incentives, we can harness the sun's energy to reduce greenhouse gas emissions and create jobs in the burgeoning solar industry.

Wind Power:

Wind power is another promising source of renewable energy, with vast potential to generate electricity in regions with strong and consistent wind resources. Wind turbines harness the kinetic energy of the wind to produce electricity, providing a clean and reliable source of power for communities across the country. By investing in wind power projects and expanding wind energy capacity, we can diversify America's energy portfolio and reduce our dependence on fossil fuels.

Hydroelectric Power:

Hydroelectric power, generated from flowing water, has long been a reliable source of renewable energy in the United States. Hydropower facilities, such as dams and hydroelectric plants, produce electricity by harnessing the energy of falling water to turn turbines and generate electricity. By investing in hydroelectric power infrastructure and modernizing existing facilities, we can maximize the potential of this clean and renewable energy source.

Energy Efficiency and Conservation:

In addition to investing in renewable energy sources, we must also prioritize energy efficiency and conservation efforts to reduce energy consumption and minimize waste. Energy efficiency measures, such as upgrading buildings, appliances, and transportation systems, can significantly reduce energy demand and lower greenhouse gas emissions. By promoting energy conservation behaviors and adopting energy-efficient technologies, we can reduce our reliance on fossil fuels and build a more sustainable energy future.

Addressing Challenges and Barriers:

Transitioning to renewable energy will not be without its challenges. From regulatory barriers and market dynamics to technological limitations and public perception, there are numerous obstacles that must be overcome to accelerate the adoption of renewable energy technologies. However, with political will, technological innovation, and public support, we can overcome these challenges and realize the full potential of renewable energy to power America's future.

Conclusion:

Transitioning to renewable energy is essential for reducing America's dependence on fossil fuels, mitigating the impacts of climate change, and building a more sustainable and resilient energy future. By investing in solar, wind, hydroelectric, and other renewable energy sources, we can create jobs, stimulate economic growth, and protect the environment for future generations. However, achieving energy independence will require concerted efforts from government, industry, and the public to overcome barriers and accelerate the transition to clean and renewable energy sources. With bold action and a commitment to innovation, we can chart a course towards a brighter and more sustainable energy future for America.

Chapter 7

Environmental Conservation

Introduction:

Environmental conservation is essential for preserving the health and well-being of our planet and future generations. From protecting natural habitats and biodiversity to mitigating climate change and reducing pollution, conservation efforts play a critical role in safeguarding the environment for all living beings. In this chapter, we will explore the importance of environmental conservation and propose strategies for promoting sustainability and resilience in the face of environmental challenges.

Addressing Climate Change:

Climate change poses one of the greatest threats to our planet and requires urgent action to mitigate its impacts and adapt to changing environmental conditions. The burning of fossil fuels, deforestation, and industrial activities have led to rising greenhouse gas emissions, resulting in global warming, sea-level rise, and extreme weather events.

To address climate change, we must transition to renewable energy sources, reduce emissions from transportation and industry, and protect natural carbon sinks such as forests and wetlands. Additionally, we must invest in climate resilience measures to prepare communities for the impacts of climate change, including stronger storms, heatwaves, and droughts.

Protecting Natural Resources:

Natural resources, such as forests, oceans, and freshwater ecosystems, provide essential services for humans and wildlife alike. However, these resources are under threat from deforestation, overfishing, pollution, and habitat destruction. Protecting and restoring natural habitats is essential for preserving biodiversity, mitigating climate change, and ensuring the health and resilience of ecosystems.

Conservation efforts may include establishing protected areas, implementing sustainable land management practices, and promoting habitat restoration initiatives. Additionally, we must address the root causes of environmental degradation, such as unsustainable agriculture, urban sprawl, and industrial pollution, through policy reforms and public education campaigns.

Promoting Sustainability:

Sustainability is the key to ensuring that future generations can meet their needs without compromising the ability of future generations to do the same. Sustainable development balances economic, social, and environmental considerations to promote prosperity while protecting the planet. By adopting sustainable practices in areas such as energy, transportation, and agriculture, we can reduce our ecological footprint and build a more resilient and equitable society.

One way to promote sustainability is through the adoption of circular economy principles, which seek to minimize waste and maximize resource efficiency by reusing, recycling, and repurposing materials. Additionally, sustainable agriculture practices, such as organic farming and agroforestry, can help protect soil health, conserve water, and reduce greenhouse gas emissions.

Engaging Communities:

Environmental conservation requires the collective effort of governments, businesses, communities, and individuals working together to protect and preserve the natural world. Community engagement is essential for raising awareness, building support, and mobilizing action on environmental issues. By empowering communities to participate in conservation efforts, we can create a sense of ownership and responsibility for the environment and foster a culture of stewardship and sustainability.

Community-based conservation initiatives may include citizen science programs, environmental education initiatives, and grassroots advocacy campaigns. Additionally, partnerships between government agencies, non-profit organizations, and local communities can leverage local knowledge and resources to achieve conservation goals and address environmental challenges.

Conclusion:

Environmental conservation is essential for ensuring the health and well-being of our planet and future generations. By addressing climate change, protecting natural resources, promoting sustainability, and engaging communities, we can build a more resilient and sustainable world for all living beings. However, achieving environmental conservation will require collective action, political will, and a commitment to protecting the planet for future generations. With bold action and a shared vision, we can preserve the beauty and diversity of our natural world for generations to come.

Chapter 8

Immigration Reform

Introduction:

Immigration has been a central aspect of American identity and history, contributing to the nation's cultural diversity, economic prosperity, and social fabric. However, America's immigration system is in need of comprehensive reform to address longstanding challenges and ensure fairness, security, and opportunity for immigrants and native-born citizens alike. In this chapter, we will explore the complexities of immigration reform and propose strategies for creating a more just and humane immigration system.

The Current Immigration System:

America's immigration system is a complex web of laws, regulations, and agencies that govern who can enter the country, how long they can stay, and under what conditions they can work and live in the United States. The system is characterized by bureaucratic inefficiencies, long wait times, and a patchwork of policies that can be confusing and difficult to navigate for immigrants and their families.

One of the biggest challenges facing America's immigration system is the presence of millions of undocumented immigrants living and working in the country. These individuals often face significant barriers to accessing basic services such as healthcare, education, and legal representation, and live in constant fear of deportation.

Reforming Immigration Policies:

To address these challenges and create a more equitable and humane immigration system, we must pursue comprehensive reforms that address the needs of both immigrants and native-born citizens. This includes providing a pathway to citizenship for undocumented immigrants, modernizing legal immigration channels, and strengthening border security and enforcement measures.

Pathway to Citizenship:

One of the most pressing issues in immigration reform is the status of undocumented immigrants living in the United States. These individuals, many of whom have lived in the country for years or even decades, contribute to their communities and the economy but live in constant fear of deportation. Providing a pathway to citizenship for undocumented immigrants would not only recognize their contributions but also promote integration, stability, and fairness in our immigration system.

A pathway to citizenship could include requirements such as paying taxes, passing background checks, and demonstrating English proficiency and knowledge of American civics. Additionally, it could prioritize individuals with strong ties to the United States, such as those with family members who are citizens or permanent residents, or those who have served in the military or are essential workers.

Modernizing Legal Immigration Channels:

In addition to addressing the status of undocumented immigrants, we must also modernize legal immigration channels to ensure that the system is fair, efficient, and responsive to the needs of the economy and society. This includes streamlining visa processing, reducing backlogs, and updating visa categories to reflect changing labor market demands.

One way to modernize legal immigration channels is to create new pathways for immigrants with skills, talents, and entrepreneurial ambitions to come to the United States. This could include expanding visa categories for high-skilled workers, entrepreneurs, and investors, and creating new opportunities for temporary or seasonal workers in industries such as agriculture, hospitality, and healthcare.

Strengthening Border Security:

While addressing the status of undocumented immigrants and modernizing legal immigration channels are important components of immigration reform, we must also prioritize border security and enforcement measures to ensure the integrity of our immigration system and protect national security.

This could include investments in technology and infrastructure to secure the border, such as surveillance cameras, drones, and border fencing. Additionally, it could involve enhancing coordination and cooperation between federal, state, and local law enforcement agencies to detect and apprehend individuals who pose a threat to public safety or national security.

Promoting Economic and Cultural Contributions:

Immigrants have long been essential contributors to America's economy, culture, and society. They start businesses, create jobs, pay taxes, and enrich our communities with their diverse perspectives, talents, and traditions. Recognizing and celebrating the contributions of immigrants is essential for fostering inclusivity, promoting social cohesion, and building a stronger and more resilient nation.

Conclusion:

Immigration reform is essential for ensuring that America's immigration system is fair, efficient, and responsive to the needs of immigrants and native-born citizens alike. By providing a pathway to citizenship for undocumented immigrants, modernizing legal immigration channels, and strengthening border security and enforcement measures, we can create a more just and humane immigration system that reflects America's values of fairness, opportunity, and diversity. However, achieving meaningful immigration reform will require political will, bipartisan cooperation, and a commitment to upholding the rights and dignity of all individuals, regardless of their immigration status. With bold action and a shared vision, we can create a more just and inclusive society that benefits immigrants, native-born citizens, and future generations alike.

Chapter 9

Criminal Justice Reform

Introduction:

The criminal justice system plays a crucial role in maintaining public safety, upholding the rule of law, and promoting justice and fairness in society. However, America's criminal justice system is in need of comprehensive reform to address systemic issues such as racial disparities, mass incarceration, and over-criminalization. In this chapter, we will explore the complexities of criminal justice reform and propose strategies for creating a more equitable and effective system.

Understanding the Criminal Justice System:

The criminal justice system is composed of various agencies and institutions, including law enforcement, courts, and corrections, that work together to investigate, prosecute, and adjudicate criminal offenses. While these components play distinct roles, they are interconnected and interdependent, shaping the outcomes and experiences of individuals who come into contact with the system.

One of the key challenges facing America's criminal justice system is the over-reliance on punitive measures such as incarceration, which often fail to address the underlying causes of crime and can perpetuate cycles of poverty, violence, and recidivism. Additionally, racial and socioeconomic disparities in the criminal justice system undermine public trust and confidence in the fairness and legitimacy of the system.

Reforming Policing Practices:

Law enforcement agencies are the frontline of the criminal justice system, responsible for enforcing laws, maintaining public order, and protecting communities from crime and violence. However, policing practices can vary widely across jurisdictions, leading to disparities in how communities are policed and how individuals are treated by law enforcement officers.

To address these disparities and promote accountability and transparency in policing, we must pursue reforms that prioritize community engagement, de-escalation techniques, and nonviolent approaches to law enforcement. This may include implementing training programs on implicit bias and cultural competence, adopting body-worn cameras and other accountability measures, and establishing civilian oversight boards to review complaints and incidents of misconduct.

Promoting Alternatives to Incarceration:

In recent decades, America has witnessed a dramatic rise in incarceration rates, fueled by harsh sentencing laws, mandatory minimums, and tough-on-crime policies. As a result, the United States now incarcerates more people per capita than any other country in the world, with profound social and economic consequences for individuals, families, and communities.

To address the over-reliance on incarceration and reduce the burden on the criminal justice system, we must promote alternatives to incarceration that prioritize rehabilitation, treatment, and reintegration for individuals involved in the justice system. This may include diversion programs for nonviolent offenders, drug courts for individuals struggling with substance abuse, and restorative justice practices that focus on repairing harm and addressing the root causes of crime.

Addressing Racial Disparities:

Racial disparities pervade every stage of the criminal justice system, from policing and arrest practices to sentencing and incarceration rates. Black and brown communities are disproportionately impacted by over-policing, harsh sentencing, and disparate treatment within the justice system, leading to profound inequities in outcomes and experiences.

To address racial disparities in the criminal justice system, we must confront the legacy of systemic racism and discrimination that has shaped law enforcement policies and practices. This may include reforms such as ending racial profiling, eliminating cash bail, and promoting implicit bias training for law enforcement officers and criminal justice professionals. Additionally, we must invest in community-based initiatives that address the social determinants of crime and promote economic opportunity, education, and health equity in marginalized communities.

Conclusion:

Criminal justice reform is essential for creating a more equitable, effective, and humane system that promotes public safety, upholds the rule of law, and protects the rights and dignity of all individuals. By reforming policing practices, promoting alternatives to incarceration, and addressing racial disparities, we can build a criminal justice system that reflects America's values of fairness, justice, and equality. However, achieving meaningful criminal justice reform will require political will, bipartisan cooperation, and a commitment to upholding the rights and dignity of all individuals, regardless of their involvement in the justice system. With bold action and a shared vision, we can create a criminal justice system that serves the needs of communities, promotes public safety, and upholds the principles of justice and fairness for all.

Chapter 10

Education Reform: A Blueprint for the Future

Introduction:

Education is the cornerstone of a thriving society, shaping the minds and futures of individuals and communities. Yet, America's education system faces significant challenges that hinder its ability to prepare students for the demands of the 21st century. In this chapter, we will outline a comprehensive blueprint for education reform, addressing key areas such as access, equity, quality, and innovation.

Access to Quality Education:

Ensuring access to quality education for all students is essential for promoting equity and opportunity in society. However, disparities in access to resources, opportunities, and support persist, particularly for students from marginalized communities. To address these disparities, we must prioritize investments in early childhood education, K-12 schools, and post-secondary education, as well as initiatives to support teachers and improve school environments.

Early Childhood Education:

Early childhood education is critical for laying the foundation for lifelong learning and success. Research has shown that high-quality early childhood education programs can have significant benefits for children's cognitive, social, and emotional development, particularly for children from low-income families. To expand access to early childhood education, we must invest in universal pre-K programs, increase funding for Head Start and Early Head Start, and support initiatives that promote parent engagement and family support.

K-12 Education:

America's K-12 education system is the primary vehicle for preparing students for college, careers, and civic engagement. However, many schools face challenges such as inadequate funding, outdated curricula, and disparities in resources and opportunities. To improve K-12 education, we must prioritize reforms that promote equity, excellence, and innovation in schools, including increasing funding for high-needs schools, supporting teacher professional development, and implementing evidence-based practices that support student learning and achievement.

Post-Secondary Education:

Access to post-secondary education is essential for preparing students for success in today's knowledge-based economy. However, rising tuition costs, student debt, and barriers to access hinder many students from pursuing higher education. To expand access to post-secondary education, we must invest in financial aid programs, support community colleges and vocational training programs, and promote initiatives that help students succeed in college and beyond.

Supporting Teachers and Improving School Environments:

Teachers play a crucial role in shaping the learning experiences and outcomes of students. Yet, many teachers face significant challenges, including low salaries, inadequate resources, and lack of support. Additionally, schools themselves often grapple with issues such as overcrowding, outdated facilities, and safety concerns. To support teachers and improve school environments, we must invest in recruiting and retaining high-quality educators, providing them with the training, resources, and support they need to succeed. This may include initiatives to raise teacher salaries, reduce class sizes, and modernize school facilities. Additionally, efforts to promote school safety and create supportive and inclusive school environments are essential for fostering student success.

Promoting Equity and Inclusion:

Achieving equity and inclusion in education requires addressing systemic barriers and disparities that limit access and opportunity for marginalized students. This includes confronting issues such as racial segregation, unequal funding, and disciplinary practices that disproportionately impact students of color, students with disabilities, and other marginalized groups. To promote equity and inclusion, we must prioritize policies and initiatives that dismantle barriers, promote diversity and representation, and ensure that all students have access to high-quality education and opportunities for success.

Innovation and Excellence:

Innovation is essential for driving continuous improvement and excellence in education. By embracing new ideas, technologies, and approaches to teaching and learning, we can create schools that are responsive, adaptive, and effective in meeting the needs of diverse learners. This may include initiatives to promote personalized learning, project-based learning, and competency-based education, as well as investments in educational technology and digital resources that enhance student engagement and outcomes.

Conclusion:

Education reform is essential for ensuring that all students have access to the knowledge, skills, and opportunities they need to succeed in the 21st century. By prioritizing investments in early childhood education, K-12 schools, and post-secondary education, supporting teachers, promoting equity and inclusion, and fostering innovation and excellence, we can create a more equitable, effective, and responsive education system that prepares students for success in college, careers, and civic life. However, achieving meaningful education reform will require political will, bipartisan cooperation, and a commitment to investing in America's future. With bold action and a shared vision, we can build a brighter future for all students and ensure that every child has the opportunity to achieve their full potential.

Chapter 11

Economic Empowerment and Opportunity

Introduction:

Economic empowerment and opportunity are fundamental pillars of a thriving society, providing individuals and communities with the means to achieve financial security, upward mobility, and a better quality of life. However, America's economy is characterized by disparities in income, wealth, and opportunity that perpetuate inequality and limit social mobility. In this chapter, we will explore strategies for promoting economic empowerment and opportunity for all Americans, regardless of their background or circumstances.

Understanding Economic Inequality:

Economic inequality is a pervasive and complex issue that affects individuals and communities across the country. While America is one of the wealthiest nations in the world, many Americans struggle to make ends meet and face barriers to economic opportunity. Disparities in income, wealth, and access to resources perpetuate cycles of poverty and limit social mobility, particularly for marginalized communities.

One of the key drivers of economic inequality is structural barriers such as discrimination, systemic racism, and unequal access to education, employment, and housing. Additionally, changes in the economy, such as globalization, automation, and technological advancements, have reshaped the labor market and created new challenges for workers and businesses alike.

Promoting Economic Empowerment:

Economic empowerment is essential for giving individuals and communities the tools, resources, and opportunities they need to achieve financial security and independence. This includes strategies to increase access to education and training, promote entrepreneurship and small business development, and support workforce development initiatives that prepare individuals for the jobs of the future.

Access to Education and Training:

Education is one of the most powerful tools for promoting economic empowerment and opportunity. By investing in education and training programs that equip individuals with the knowledge, skills, and credentials they need to succeed in the workforce, we can expand access to economic opportunity and reduce disparities in income and wealth.

This may include initiatives such as universal pre-K, affordable higher education and vocational training programs, and workforce development initiatives that provide job training and support services to individuals seeking to enter or reenter the workforce. Additionally, efforts to address disparities in access to quality education and resources, particularly for marginalized communities, are essential for promoting equity and inclusion in the economy.

Promoting Entrepreneurship and Small Business Development:

Entrepreneurship is a powerful driver of economic growth, innovation, and job creation. By promoting entrepreneurship and small business development, we can create opportunities for individuals to build wealth, create jobs, and contribute to the vitality of their communities.

This may include initiatives such as access to capital and credit, technical assistance and mentorship programs, and support for minority-owned and women-owned businesses. Additionally, efforts to streamline regulations, reduce bureaucratic barriers, and promote inclusive economic development strategies can help create a more favorable environment for entrepreneurship and small business growth.

Supporting Workforce Development:

Workforce development initiatives are essential for preparing individuals for the jobs of the future and ensuring that businesses have access to a skilled and qualified workforce. By investing in workforce development programs that provide training, education, and support services to workers, we can address skill gaps, promote career advancement, and support economic growth and competitiveness.

This may include initiatives such as apprenticeship programs, on-the-job training initiatives, and sector-based partnerships that align training programs with the needs of employers. Additionally, efforts to promote diversity, equity, and inclusion in the workforce, such as targeted recruitment and retention strategies, are essential for creating an economy that works for everyone.

Conclusion:

Economic empowerment and opportunity are essential for creating a more equitable, inclusive, and prosperous society. By investing in education and training, promoting entrepreneurship and small business development, and supporting workforce development initiatives, we can create opportunities for all Americans to achieve financial security, upward mobility, and a better quality of life. However, achieving meaningful economic empowerment will require political will, bipartisan cooperation, and a commitment to addressing the root causes of economic inequality. With bold action

and a shared vision, we can build an economy that works
for everyone and ensures that all Americans have the
opportunity to achieve their full potential.

Chapter 12

Social Justice and Equity

Introduction:

Social justice and equity are essential principles for
building a fair, inclusive, and compassionate society
where all individuals have the opportunity to thrive.
However, systemic injustices and disparities based on
race, ethnicity, gender, sexuality, disability, and
socioeconomic status persist in America, undermining
the promise of equality and justice for all. In this chapter,
we will explore strategies for advancing social justice
and equity and dismantling systems of oppression and
discrimination.

Understanding Social Injustice:

Social injustice refers to the unfair distribution of
resources, opportunities, and rights in society, often

perpetuated by systemic biases, discrimination, and structural barriers. Individuals and communities experience social injustice in various forms, including unequal access to education, healthcare, housing, employment, and criminal justice, among others.

One of the key drivers of social injustice is systemic racism, which has historically marginalized and oppressed communities of color and perpetuated disparities in outcomes and opportunities. Additionally, other forms of oppression, such as sexism, homophobia, transphobia, ableism, and classism, intersect and compound to exacerbate inequality and marginalization for individuals with multiple marginalized identities.

Promoting Social Justice and Equity:

Promoting social justice and equity requires confronting systemic injustices and dismantling systems of oppression and discrimination that perpetuate inequality and marginalization. This includes advocating for policy reforms, advancing social movements, and promoting cultural shifts that center the voices and experiences of marginalized communities and promote equality and justice for all.

Addressing Systemic Racism:

Systemic racism is deeply entrenched in America's institutions and structures, perpetuating disparities in education, healthcare, housing, employment, and criminal justice. To address systemic racism, we must confront its root causes and dismantle systems and policies that perpetuate racial inequality and injustice.

This may include initiatives such as criminal justice reform, police accountability measures, equitable funding for schools, affordable housing initiatives, and initiatives to address racial disparities in healthcare access and outcomes. Additionally, efforts to promote racial equity and inclusion in all sectors of society, including business, government, and education, are essential for creating a more just and equitable society for all.

Advancing LGBTQ+ Rights:

Lesbian, gay, bisexual, transgender, and queer (LGBTQ+) individuals continue to face discrimination and marginalization in many areas of society, including employment, housing, healthcare, and education. To advance LGBTQ+ rights and promote equality and inclusion, we must advocate for policies and initiatives that protect the rights and dignity of LGBTQ+ individuals and address the root causes of discrimination and stigma.

This may include initiatives such as nondiscrimination laws, hate crime legislation, transgender-inclusive healthcare policies, and initiatives to promote LGBTQ+ visibility and representation in media, education, and government. Additionally, efforts to address the unique needs and challenges faced by LGBTQ+ youth, elders, and communities of color are essential for promoting equity and justice for all LGBTQ+ individuals.

Promoting Gender Equity:

Gender inequality continues to persist in many areas of society, including the workplace, politics, and the home. Women and gender-nonconforming individuals face disparities in pay, representation, and access to resources and opportunities, perpetuated by systemic biases and discrimination.

To promote gender equity, we must advocate for policies and initiatives that address the root causes of gender inequality and promote equality and empowerment for all genders. This may include initiatives such as pay equity laws, paid family leave policies, initiatives to promote women's leadership and representation in politics and business, and efforts to challenge harmful gender norms and stereotypes.

Conclusion:

Social justice and equity are essential principles for creating a fair, inclusive, and compassionate society where all individuals have the opportunity to thrive. By confronting systemic injustices, dismantling systems of oppression and discrimination, and promoting policies and initiatives that center the voices and experiences of marginalized communities, we can create a more just and equitable world for all. However, achieving meaningful social justice and equity will require political will, grassroots activism, and a commitment to challenging and changing the status quo. With bold action and a shared vision, we can build a society that honors the dignity and humanity of all individuals and promotes equality, justice, and liberation for all.

Chapter 13

Healthcare Reform: Building a Healthier Nation

Introduction:

Healthcare is a fundamental human right, essential for promoting well-being, economic prosperity, and social equity. However, America's healthcare system is plagued by inefficiencies, inequities, and soaring costs that limit access to care and contribute to disparities in health outcomes. In this chapter, we will explore strategies for reforming the healthcare system to ensure that all Americans have access to affordable, high-quality care and promote health and well-being for all.

Understanding the Healthcare Crisis:

America's healthcare system faces a myriad of challenges, including rising costs, unequal access to care, and disparities in health outcomes based on factors such as race, ethnicity, income, and geography. Despite spending more per capita on healthcare than any other country, the United States lags behind other developed nations in key indicators such as life expectancy, infant mortality, and preventable deaths.

One of the key drivers of the healthcare crisis is the lack of universal healthcare coverage, which leaves millions of Americans uninsured or underinsured and unable to access essential medical services. Additionally, the fragmentation of the healthcare system, with multiple payers, providers, and regulators, contributes to administrative complexity, inefficiency, and waste.

Reforming the Healthcare System:

To address the challenges facing America's healthcare system, we must pursue comprehensive reforms that prioritize affordability, accessibility, and quality of care for all Americans. This includes expanding access to healthcare coverage, controlling costs, promoting preventive care and public health initiatives, and addressing disparities in health outcomes and access to care.

Universal Healthcare Coverage:

Universal healthcare coverage is essential for ensuring that all Americans have access to essential medical services, regardless of their income, employment status, or health status. By guaranteeing access to comprehensive healthcare coverage for all residents, we can promote health equity, financial security, and peace of mind for individuals and families.

One way to achieve universal healthcare coverage is through a single-payer healthcare system, in which the government provides health insurance to all residents and pays for healthcare services through a single, publicly funded program. This model, commonly known as Medicare for All, would eliminate private insurance companies and streamline administrative processes, reducing overhead costs and administrative complexity.

Controlling Healthcare Costs:

Controlling healthcare costs is essential for making healthcare more affordable and sustainable for individuals, families, businesses, and the government. Rising healthcare costs strain household budgets, burden businesses, and contribute to the growing federal deficit, limiting investments in other critical priorities such as education, infrastructure, and social services.

To control healthcare costs, we must address the root causes of cost growth, including inefficiencies, waste, and excessive prices for medical services, prescription drugs, and administrative expenses. This may include initiatives such as negotiating drug prices, promoting value-based care and payment models, investing in preventive care and public health initiatives, and implementing measures to reduce administrative overhead and paperwork burdens on providers.

Promoting Preventive Care and Public Health:

Preventive care and public health initiatives are essential for promoting health and well-being, preventing disease and disability, and reducing healthcare costs. By investing in preventive care services, such as screenings, vaccinations, and health education programs, we can identify health risks early, intervene proactively, and improve health outcomes for individuals and communities.

Additionally, promoting public health initiatives, such as smoking cessation programs, healthy eating campaigns, and initiatives to address social determinants of health, can help reduce the burden of chronic diseases and improve population health. By addressing the underlying factors that contribute to poor health outcomes, such as poverty, inequality, and lack of access to nutritious food and safe housing, we can create healthier, more resilient communities.

Addressing Disparities in Health Outcomes:

Disparities in health outcomes based on race, ethnicity, income, and geography persist in America, perpetuated by systemic racism, discrimination, and unequal access to care. To address these disparities, we must confront the root causes of health inequities and promote policies and initiatives that promote health equity and social justice.

This may include initiatives such as expanding access to culturally competent care, increasing investments in community health centers and safety-net hospitals serving underserved communities, and addressing social determinants of health such as poverty, housing instability, and environmental pollution. Additionally, efforts to diversify the healthcare workforce and promote health equity research and data collection are essential for advancing equity and justice in healthcare.

Conclusion:

Healthcare reform is essential for ensuring that all Americans have access to affordable, high-quality care and promoting health and well-being for all. By expanding access to healthcare coverage, controlling costs, promoting preventive care and public health initiatives, and addressing disparities in health outcomes, we can build a healthier, more equitable nation. However, achieving meaningful healthcare reform will require political will, bipartisan cooperation, and a commitment to putting the health and well-being of individuals and communities first. With bold action and a shared vision, we can create a healthcare system that works for everyone and ensures that all Americans have the opportunity to lead healthy, fulfilling lives.

Chapter 14

Environmental Justice and Sustainability

Introduction:

Environmental justice and sustainability are critical components of a healthy and equitable society, ensuring that all individuals and communities have access to clean air, water, and natural resources, and are protected from environmental harm. However, systemic injustices and disparities based on race, income, and geography often result in marginalized communities bearing the brunt of environmental pollution and degradation. In this chapter, we will explore strategies for advancing environmental justice and sustainability to create a more equitable and resilient world for all.

Understanding Environmental Injustice:

Environmental injustice refers to the disproportionate burden of environmental hazards and pollution borne by marginalized communities, including communities of color, low-income communities, and indigenous communities. These communities are often located near industrial facilities, waste sites, and other sources of pollution, exposing residents to higher levels of toxins and pollutants and increasing their risk of adverse health outcomes.

Environmental injustice is rooted in systemic racism, discrimination, and unequal access to resources and political power, which result in marginalized communities bearing a disproportionate share of the environmental harm caused by industrial pollution, hazardous waste, and climate change impacts. Additionally, historical and ongoing policies and practices, such as redlining and zoning laws, have perpetuated environmental disparities and limited opportunities for affected communities to advocate for their rights and interests.

Advancing Environmental Justice:

Advancing environmental justice requires confronting systemic injustices and addressing the root causes of environmental disparities, including racism, inequality, and political marginalization. This includes promoting policies and initiatives that center the voices and experiences of affected communities, prioritize equitable access to environmental resources and protections, and promote sustainable and resilient development practices.

One of the key principles of environmental justice is the "polluter pays" principle, which holds polluters accountable for the environmental harm they cause and ensures that affected communities have access to remedies and restitution. This may include initiatives such as enforcing environmental regulations, holding polluters accountable for cleanup and remediation efforts, and providing communities with the resources and support they need to address environmental hazards and protect their health and well-being.

Promoting Environmental Sustainability:

Environmental sustainability is essential for ensuring that present and future generations have access to clean air, water, and natural resources, and can thrive in harmony with the natural world. By promoting sustainable development practices, reducing resource consumption and waste generation, and investing in renewable energy and conservation efforts, we can build a more resilient and equitable world for all.

One way to promote environmental sustainability is through the adoption of renewable energy sources such as solar, wind, and hydroelectric power, which reduce reliance on fossil fuels and mitigate climate change impacts. Additionally, promoting energy efficiency measures, such as building retrofits and transportation upgrades, can reduce greenhouse gas emissions, lower energy costs, and create jobs in clean energy industries.

Protecting Natural Resources:

Protecting natural resources is essential for preserving biodiversity, ecosystem health, and the ecological services that sustain life on Earth. By conserving forests, wetlands, and other natural habitats, protecting endangered species, and promoting sustainable land management practices, we can safeguard the health and resilience of ecosystems and ensure that future generations can enjoy the benefits of a healthy environment.

This may include initiatives such as establishing protected areas and wildlife corridors, promoting sustainable agriculture and forestry practices, and restoring degraded ecosystems through reforestation, habitat restoration, and conservation initiatives. Additionally, efforts to address environmental threats such as pollution, deforestation, and habitat destruction are essential for protecting natural resources and promoting environmental sustainability.

Conclusion:

Environmental justice and sustainability are essential for creating a more equitable, resilient, and sustainable world for all. By confronting systemic injustices, addressing the root causes of environmental disparities, and promoting policies and initiatives that center the voices and experiences of affected communities, we can build a future where everyone has access to clean air, water, and natural resources, and can thrive in harmony with the natural world. However, achieving meaningful progress on environmental justice and sustainability will require political will, grassroots activism, and a commitment to upholding the rights and dignity of all individuals and communities. With bold action and a shared vision, we can create a world where environmental justice and sustainability are at the forefront of decision-making, and where every individual and community have the opportunity to live in a healthy and thriving environment.

Chapter 15

Technology and Innovation for the Future

Introduction:

Technology and innovation have the power to transform society, drive economic growth, and address some of the most pressing challenges facing humanity. From advancements in artificial intelligence and renewable energy to breakthroughs in healthcare and transportation, technology has the potential to revolutionize how we live, work, and interact with the world around us. In this chapter, we will explore the role of technology and innovation in shaping the future and propose strategies for harnessing their potential to create a more prosperous, sustainable, and equitable world for all.

The Promise of Technology:

Technology has the power to improve lives, expand opportunities, and solve complex problems that have long plagued humanity. From enhancing communication and connectivity to advancing healthcare and education, technology has the potential to unlock new possibilities and empower individuals and communities to thrive in the 21st century.

One of the key promises of technology is its ability to democratize access to information and resources, leveling the playing field and empowering individuals from diverse backgrounds to participate in the global economy and society. Additionally, technology can drive innovation and productivity, creating new industries, jobs, and opportunities for economic growth and development.

Advancements in Artificial Intelligence:

Artificial intelligence (AI) holds the potential to revolutionize nearly every aspect of human life, from healthcare and transportation to finance and entertainment. By leveraging machine learning algorithms and big data analytics, AI can help improve decision-making, automate repetitive tasks, and unlock insights and efficiencies that were previously inaccessible.

In healthcare, for example, AI-powered diagnostic tools and predictive analytics can help improve patient outcomes, reduce medical errors, and lower healthcare costs. In transportation, self-driving cars and smart transportation systems have the potential to reduce traffic congestion, improve safety, and increase access to mobility for underserved communities.

However, the widespread adoption of AI also raises concerns about ethics, privacy, and equity. It is essential to ensure that AI technologies are developed and deployed responsibly, with safeguards in place to protect against bias, discrimination, and unintended consequences. Additionally, efforts to promote diversity and inclusion in the tech industry are essential for ensuring that AI technologies reflect the needs and interests of all individuals and communities.

Advancements in Renewable Energy:

Renewable energy technologies, such as solar, wind, and hydropower, hold the potential to transform the way we produce and consume energy, reducing reliance on fossil fuels and mitigating the impacts of climate change. By harnessing the power of the sun, wind, and water, we can create a more sustainable and resilient energy system that reduces greenhouse gas emissions, improves air quality, and promotes energy independence.

In recent years, advancements in renewable energy technologies have led to significant cost reductions and scalability, making clean energy sources increasingly competitive with traditional fossil fuels. Additionally, innovations in energy storage, grid management, and smart infrastructure are helping to overcome challenges such as intermittency and variability, making renewable energy more reliable and accessible.

Promoting Access to Technology and Digital Inclusion:

While technology has the potential to empower individuals and communities, disparities in access to technology and digital skills persist, particularly for marginalized communities and underserved populations. To promote digital inclusion and bridge the digital divide, we must prioritize initiatives that expand access to affordable broadband internet, devices, and digital literacy training programs.

This may include initiatives such as community broadband projects, public-private partnerships, and subsidies for low-income households to access affordable internet service. Additionally, efforts to promote digital literacy and skills training, particularly in underserved communities, are essential for ensuring that all individuals have the knowledge and capabilities to fully participate in the digital economy and society.

Ethical Considerations and Responsible Innovation:

As technology continues to advance, it is essential to consider the ethical implications of emerging technologies and their potential impacts on society. Issues such as data privacy, algorithmic bias, and autonomous decision-making raise complex ethical questions that require careful consideration and responsible governance.

To promote ethical innovation and ensure that technology serves the greater good, we must prioritize transparency, accountability, and human-centered design principles in the development and deployment of new technologies. Additionally, efforts to engage diverse stakeholders, including policymakers, researchers, and community representatives, are essential for fostering dialogue, building consensus, and addressing ethical concerns in a collaborative and inclusive manner.

Conclusion:

Technology and innovation have the power to shape the future and create a more prosperous, sustainable, and equitable world for all. By harnessing the potential of emerging technologies such as artificial intelligence and renewable energy, promoting access to technology and digital inclusion, and considering the ethical implications of technological advancements, we can build a future where technology serves the needs and interests of all individuals and communities. However, achieving meaningful progress on technology and innovation will require political will, public-private collaboration, and a commitment to advancing equity, ethics, and social responsibility in the development and deployment of new technologies. With bold action and a shared vision, we can harness the power of technology to build a brighter future for generations to come.

Chapter 16

Global Leadership and Cooperation

Introduction:

In an interconnected world facing complex challenges such as climate change, pandemics, and economic instability, global leadership and cooperation are essential for addressing shared problems and advancing common goals. As a leading global power, the United States has a responsibility to engage with other nations, uphold international norms and agreements, and promote peace, prosperity, and security for all. In this chapter, we will explore the importance of global leadership and cooperation and outline strategies for strengthening America's role on the world stage.

The Importance of Global Leadership:

Global leadership is essential for addressing transnational challenges that transcend borders and require collective action to solve. From promoting peace and security to advancing human rights and sustainable development, global leadership enables nations to work together to tackle shared problems and seize opportunities for progress and prosperity.

As a global leader, the United States has historically played a central role in shaping international norms and institutions, from the United Nations and NATO to the World Trade Organization and the Paris Agreement on climate change. By leveraging its economic, military, and diplomatic resources, the United States has helped shape the global order and advance its values and interests on the world stage.

However, in recent years, the United States has faced criticism for retreating from its global leadership role, undermining international agreements, and adopting an isolationist stance on key issues such as trade, climate change, and immigration. To restore America's global leadership and credibility, it is essential to reaffirm commitment to multilateralism, strengthen partnerships with allies and partners, and promote cooperation and dialogue on pressing global challenges.

Promoting Multilateralism and Diplomacy:

Multilateralism is the cornerstone of effective global governance, enabling nations to pool resources, share burdens, and coordinate responses to complex challenges. By engaging with multilateral institutions such as the United Nations, the World Health Organization, and the International Monetary Fund, the United States can amplify its influence, leverage collective action, and promote international cooperation on a wide range of issues.

Diplomacy is another essential tool for advancing global leadership and resolving conflicts through peaceful means. By prioritizing diplomacy and dialogue over coercion and confrontation, the United States can build trust, foster understanding, and promote cooperation with other nations. Additionally, investing in diplomatic corps and diplomatic training programs can strengthen America's diplomatic capabilities and enable skilled diplomats to navigate complex global challenges and negotiations effectively.

Addressing Global Challenges:

From climate change and pandemics to terrorism and nuclear proliferation, the world faces a myriad of complex challenges that require collective action and global cooperation to address. As a global leader, the United States has a responsibility to work with other nations to find solutions to these challenges and promote peace, security, and prosperity for all.

One of the most urgent global challenges facing humanity is climate change, which threatens to disrupt ecosystems, exacerbate extreme weather events, and undermine global stability and prosperity. By recommitting to the Paris Agreement and adopting ambitious climate targets, the United States can demonstrate leadership on climate action and encourage other nations to follow suit.

Additionally, addressing global health crises such as pandemics requires coordinated international efforts to prevent, detect, and respond to outbreaks and ensure equitable access to vaccines and treatments. By supporting initiatives such as the World Health Organization's COVAX facility, the United States can help strengthen global health security and build resilience against future pandemics.

Promoting Human Rights and Democracy:

Promoting human rights and democracy is essential for advancing global peace, stability, and prosperity. By championing human rights principles such as freedom of speech, press, and assembly, the United States can support civil society, empower marginalized communities, and hold authoritarian regimes accountable for human rights abuses.

Additionally, supporting democratic institutions and processes, such as free and fair elections, independent judiciaries, and transparent governance, can help strengthen democracy and rule of law around the world. By promoting democracy and human rights, the United States can build alliances with like-minded nations, foster stability and prosperity, and counter authoritarianism and extremism.

Conclusion:

Global leadership and cooperation are essential for addressing shared challenges and advancing common goals in an interconnected world. By reaffirming commitment to multilateralism, promoting diplomacy and dialogue, addressing global challenges such as climate change and pandemics, and championing human rights and democracy, the United States can strengthen its role as a global leader and contribute to a more peaceful, prosperous, and sustainable world for all. However, achieving meaningful progress on global leadership and cooperation will require political will, diplomatic skill, and a commitment to upholding international norms and values. With bold action and a shared vision, the United States can build a future where nations work together to tackle shared challenges and build a better world for generations to come.

Chapter 17

Strengthening National Security in a Changing World

Introduction:

National security is a paramount concern for any nation, encompassing efforts to protect its citizens, territory, and interests from external threats and internal challenges. In an increasingly interconnected and unpredictable world, the United States faces a range of complex security threats, from terrorism and cyberattacks to nuclear proliferation and great power competition. In this chapter, we will explore strategies for strengthening national security in a changing world and safeguarding America's interests and values.

Understanding National Security Threats:

National security threats are diverse and evolving, encompassing a wide range of challenges that require comprehensive and adaptable responses. These threats can emanate from state actors, such as rival nations and hostile regimes, as well as non-state actors, such as terrorist groups, criminal organizations, and cyber hackers.

One of the most pressing national security threats facing the United States is terrorism, which remains a persistent and evolving threat to global stability and security. While significant progress has been made in degrading terrorist organizations such as al-Qaeda and ISIS, the threat of terrorism persists, with new groups and lone actors emerging to carry out attacks and spread violence and fear.

Cybersecurity is another critical national security challenge, as the proliferation of digital technologies and interconnected networks has created new vulnerabilities and opportunities for malicious actors to exploit. Cyberattacks targeting critical infrastructure, government agencies, and private sector entities pose significant risks to national security, economic stability, and public safety.

Additionally, great power competition between nations such as China, Russia, and Iran pose strategic challenges to the United States and its allies, as these countries seek to assert their influence, expand their capabilities, and challenge the existing international order.

Strategies for Strengthening National Security:

To address the complex and evolving nature of national security threats, the United States must adopt a comprehensive and integrated approach that combines military, diplomatic, economic, and technological capabilities. This includes efforts to enhance intelligence gathering and analysis, strengthen cybersecurity defenses, bolster alliances and partnerships, and promote stability and prosperity around the world.

Investing in Military Capabilities:

Maintaining a strong and capable military is essential for deterring aggression, defending against threats, and protecting America's interests and allies around the world. This includes investments in advanced weapons systems, modernization of military infrastructure, and training and readiness initiatives to ensure that the Armed Forces are prepared to respond to a range of contingencies.

Additionally, efforts to promote interoperability and cooperation with allies and partners are essential for enhancing collective defense capabilities and fostering stability and security in regions of strategic importance. By strengthening alliances such as NATO and building partnerships with like-minded nations, the United States can project strength and deter potential adversaries while promoting peace and security.

Enhancing Cybersecurity Defenses:

Cybersecurity is a critical component of national security, as cyberattacks pose significant risks to government agencies, critical infrastructure, and private sector entities. To enhance cybersecurity defenses, the United States must invest in technologies and capabilities to detect, prevent, and respond to cyber threats, as well as promote collaboration and information sharing among government agencies, industry partners, and international allies.

This may include initiatives such as enhancing the resilience of critical infrastructure, improving incident response capabilities, and promoting cybersecurity awareness and education among the public and private sectors. Additionally, efforts to deter malicious cyber actors through diplomatic, economic, and legal means are essential for holding perpetrators accountable and deterring future attacks.

Promoting Diplomacy and Conflict Resolution:

Diplomacy and conflict resolution are essential tools for addressing regional conflicts, managing geopolitical tensions, and preventing the outbreak of armed conflict. By engaging in diplomatic dialogue, promoting confidence-building measures, and supporting peace negotiations, the United States can help defuse tensions and resolve disputes through peaceful means.

Additionally, efforts to promote stability and economic development in regions affected by conflict and instability can help address the root causes of violence and extremism, reduce the risk of conflict escalation, and create conditions for peace and prosperity. This may include initiatives such as humanitarian assistance, development aid, and capacity-building programs to strengthen governance, institutions, and civil society.

Promoting Resilience and Preparedness:

Resilience and preparedness are essential for ensuring that the United States can effectively respond to and recover from national security threats and emergencies. By investing in disaster preparedness and response capabilities, enhancing resilience of critical infrastructure, and promoting community resilience and engagement, the United States can mitigate the impact of disasters and disruptions and ensure the continuity of essential services and functions.

Additionally, efforts to address emerging threats such as pandemics and climate change require proactive measures to anticipate, prevent, and mitigate their impact. By investing in public health infrastructure, disease surveillance systems, and climate resilience initiatives, the United States can build resilience against emerging threats and protect the health and well-being of its citizens.

Conclusion:

Strengthening national security is essential for safeguarding America's interests, values, and way of life in an increasingly complex and uncertain world. By adopting a comprehensive and integrated approach that combines military strength, diplomatic engagement, cybersecurity defenses, and resilience and preparedness initiatives, the United States can address the diverse and evolving nature of national security threats and promote peace, stability, and prosperity for all. However, achieving meaningful progress on national security will require political will, strategic foresight, and a commitment to upholding America's role as a global leader and defender of freedom and democracy. With bold action and a shared vision, the United States can build a safer, more secure future for generations to come.

Chapter 18

Cultivating a Culture of Innovation and Creativity

Introduction:

Innovation and creativity are the driving forces behind progress and prosperity, fueling economic growth, driving technological advancements, and solving some of the world's most pressing challenges. Cultivating a culture of innovation and creativity is essential for empowering individuals and organizations to unleash their full potential, explore new ideas, and pursue bold solutions to complex problems. In this chapter, we will explore the importance of innovation and creativity and outline strategies for fostering a culture of innovation in society.

Understanding Innovation and Creativity:

Innovation and creativity are closely intertwined concepts that involve the generation of novel ideas, products, or processes that create value and drive positive change. While innovation often refers to the application of new ideas or technologies to solve practical problems or meet market needs, creativity is the ability to generate original and imaginative ideas, insights, or solutions that break with conventional thinking and paradigms.

Innovation and creativity can take many forms, from scientific breakthroughs and technological inventions to artistic expressions and social innovations. However, they share common characteristics such as curiosity, experimentation, collaboration, and risk-taking, which are essential for pushing the boundaries of what is possible and driving progress and innovation in society.

The Importance of Innovation and Creativity:

Innovation and creativity are essential for addressing the complex challenges facing society, from climate change and public health crises to economic inequality and social injustice. By fostering a culture of innovation and creativity, individuals and organizations can develop new solutions, approaches, and technologies that improve lives, drive economic growth, and create positive social change.

Innovation and creativity are also key drivers of economic competitiveness and prosperity, as they enable businesses to develop new products and services, enter new markets, and adapt to changing consumer preferences and technological trends. Additionally, innovation and creativity are essential for fostering entrepreneurship and small business development, which are critical engines of job creation, wealth generation, and economic resilience.

Strategies for Fostering Innovation and Creativity:

To cultivate a culture of innovation and creativity, it is essential to create an environment that fosters curiosity, experimentation, collaboration, and risk-taking. This requires investment in education, research, infrastructure, and support systems that empower individuals and organizations to pursue their ideas and bring them to fruition.

Investing in Education and Lifelong Learning:

Education is the foundation of innovation and creativity, providing individuals with the knowledge, skills, and mindset they need to think critically, solve problems, and generate new ideas. By investing in education systems that emphasize creativity, critical thinking, and hands-on learning, we can empower students to become lifelong learners and innovators who are prepared to tackle the challenges of the 21st century.

This may include initiatives such as STEAM (Science, Technology, Engineering, Arts, and Mathematics) education programs, project-based learning initiatives, and experiential learning opportunities that allow students to explore their interests, pursue their passions, and develop practical skills and competencies. Additionally, efforts to promote diversity and inclusion in education are essential for ensuring that all individuals have the opportunity to participate in and contribute to innovation and creativity.

Supporting Research and Development:

Research and development (R&D) are essential drivers of innovation and technological advancement, enabling scientists, engineers, and entrepreneurs to explore new frontiers, discover new knowledge, and develop breakthrough technologies and solutions. By investing in R&D initiatives that support basic and applied research, we can drive innovation, spur economic growth, and address societal challenges.

This may include government-funded research grants, public-private partnerships, and tax incentives for businesses and universities to invest in R&D activities. Additionally, efforts to promote cross-disciplinary collaboration and knowledge sharing are essential for fostering innovation ecosystems that bring together diverse perspectives, expertise, and resources to tackle complex problems and drive progress.

Creating Supportive Ecosystems and Networks:

Creating supportive ecosystems and networks is essential for fostering innovation and entrepreneurship, providing individuals and organizations with the resources, mentorship, and connections they need to succeed. By building innovation hubs, startup accelerators, and coworking spaces, we can create environments that encourage collaboration, experimentation, and risk-taking and provide entrepreneurs with access to funding, expertise, and market opportunities.

Additionally, efforts to promote networking and knowledge exchange, such as conferences, meetups, and industry associations, are essential for connecting innovators and entrepreneurs with potential partners, investors, and customers. By building strong networks and communities, we can create a culture of innovation that empowers individuals and organizations to pursue their ideas and drive positive change in society.

Encouraging Diversity and Inclusion:

Diversity and inclusion are essential for fostering innovation and creativity, as they bring together individuals with diverse perspectives, backgrounds, and experiences that enrich the creative process and lead to more innovative and impactful solutions. By promoting diversity and inclusion in the workplace, academia, and society at large, we can create environments that value and celebrate difference and empower individuals to contribute their unique talents and insights to the innovation ecosystem.

This may include initiatives such as diversity training programs, recruitment and retention strategies to attract and retain diverse talent, and efforts to create inclusive work cultures that support collaboration, creativity, and belonging. Additionally, efforts to address systemic barriers and biases that limit opportunities for underrepresented groups, such as women, people of color, and individuals from low-income backgrounds, are essential for creating a more equitable and inclusive innovation ecosystem.

Conclusion:

Innovation and creativity are essential drivers of progress and prosperity, enabling individuals and organizations to develop new ideas, technologies, and solutions that address the challenges of our time. By fostering a culture of innovation and creativity, we can unlock human potential, drive economic growth, and create positive social change. However, achieving meaningful progress on innovation and creativity will require investment in education, research, infrastructure, and support systems that empower individuals and organizations to pursue their ideas and bring them to fruition. With bold action and a shared vision, we can cultivate a culture of innovation that unleashes the full potential of humanity and creates a brighter future for generations to come.

Chapter 19

Building Sustainable Infrastructure for the Future

Introduction:

Infrastructure forms the backbone of modern society, providing essential services and enabling economic activity, mobility, and quality of life. However, aging infrastructure, population growth, urbanization, and the impacts of climate change pose significant challenges to the resilience, efficiency, and sustainability of infrastructure systems. In this chapter, we will explore strategies for building sustainable infrastructure that meets the needs of current and future generations while addressing pressing environmental, social, and economic challenges.

Understanding Sustainable Infrastructure:

Sustainable infrastructure is designed and built with consideration for its long-term environmental, social, and economic impacts, minimizing resource consumption, reducing pollution and greenhouse gas emissions, and enhancing resilience to climate change and other disruptions. Sustainable infrastructure encompasses a wide range of sectors, including transportation, energy, water, waste management, and buildings, and requires integrated planning, design, and implementation approaches.

Key principles of sustainable infrastructure include:

1.   Resilience: Sustainable infrastructure is designed to withstand and recover from natural disasters, climate

change impacts, and other disruptions, ensuring the continuity of essential services and functions.

2.   Efficiency: Sustainable infrastructure maximizes resource use efficiency, minimizing waste, energy consumption, and environmental impacts throughout the project lifecycle.

3.   Equity: Sustainable infrastructure promotes equitable access to essential services and benefits, ensuring that all individuals and communities, particularly those historically marginalized or underserved, can benefit from infrastructure investments.

4.   Innovation: Sustainable infrastructure leverages innovative technologies, materials, and approaches to enhance performance, reduce costs, and improve outcomes.

Strategies for Building Sustainable Infrastructure:

To build sustainable infrastructure for the future, it is essential to adopt holistic and integrated approaches that consider the interconnectedness of social, environmental, and economic factors. This requires collaboration and coordination among government agencies, private sector partners, community stakeholders, and other key actors to identify priorities, set goals, and implement solutions that maximize sustainability and resilience.

Investing in Green and Resilient Transportation:

Transportation infrastructure plays a critical role in connecting people, goods, and services and driving economic growth and development. However, traditional transportation systems based on fossil fuels contribute to air pollution, greenhouse gas emissions, and traffic congestion, exacerbating environmental and public health challenges.

To build sustainable transportation infrastructure, it is essential to invest in green and resilient transportation solutions that reduce reliance on fossil fuels, promote public transit and active transportation options such as walking and cycling, and enhance the resilience of transportation networks to climate change impacts.

This may include initiatives such as expanding public transit systems, electrifying transportation fleets, investing in bike lanes and pedestrian infrastructure, and implementing smart transportation technologies to improve traffic flow and reduce emissions. Additionally, efforts to promote equitable access to transportation services and address transportation disparities in underserved communities are essential for building sustainable and inclusive transportation systems.

Promoting Renewable Energy and Sustainable Water Management:

Energy and water infrastructure are essential for meeting basic human needs, supporting economic activity, and powering modern society. However, traditional energy sources such as coal, oil, and natural gas contribute to air and water pollution, habitat destruction, and climate change, while water infrastructure faces challenges such as aging infrastructure, water scarcity, and pollution.

To build sustainable energy and water infrastructure, it is essential to promote renewable energy sources such as solar, wind, and hydropower, invest in energy efficiency and conservation measures, and promote sustainable water management practices such as water conservation, reuse, and stormwater management.

This may include initiatives such as incentivizing renewable energy deployment, implementing building energy codes and standards, investing in energy storage and grid modernization, and promoting water conservation and efficiency measures such as low-flow fixtures and drought-resistant landscaping. Additionally, efforts to address water pollution and ensure access to clean and safe drinking water for all communities are essential for building resilient and sustainable water infrastructure.

Designing Green and Resilient Buildings and Communities:

Buildings and communities are major consumers of resources and contributors to environmental degradation, accounting for a significant share of energy consumption, greenhouse gas emissions, and waste generation. However, green building and community design strategies can help reduce environmental impacts, improve indoor and outdoor air quality, and enhance quality of life for residents.

To build sustainable buildings and communities, it is essential to prioritize energy efficiency, renewable energy, and green building materials and practices that minimize resource use, reduce emissions, and enhance resilience to climate change impacts.

This may include initiatives such as adopting green building certification programs such as LEED (Leadership in Energy and Environmental Design), promoting energy-efficient building codes and standards, incentivizing green building practices through tax incentives and grants, and investing in sustainable community planning and development initiatives such as transit-oriented development, mixed-use zoning, and green infrastructure.

Conclusion:

Building sustainable infrastructure is essential for addressing the complex challenges facing society, from climate change and environmental degradation to economic inequality and social injustice. By adopting holistic and integrated approaches that prioritize resilience, efficiency, equity, and innovation, we can build infrastructure systems that meet the needs of current and future generations while protecting the planet and promoting human well-being. However, achieving meaningful progress on sustainable infrastructure will require political will, collaboration, and investment in education, research, and innovation. With bold action and a shared vision, we can build a future where sustainable infrastructure serves as the foundation for a more resilient, prosperous, and equitable world for all.

Chapter 20

Fostering Social Justice and Equity in America

Introduction:

Social justice and equity are fundamental principles that underpin a fair and just society, ensuring that all individuals have access to opportunities, resources, and rights regardless of their race, ethnicity, gender, socioeconomic status, or other characteristics. However, systemic injustices and disparities persist in America, perpetuating inequality, discrimination, and marginalization for millions of individuals and communities. In this chapter, we will explore strategies for fostering social justice and equity in America and building a more inclusive, equitable, and just society for all.

Understanding Social Injustice and Inequality:

Social injustice and inequality manifest in various forms, including economic inequality, racial discrimination, gender inequality, and disparities in access to education, healthcare, housing, and criminal justice. These disparities are often rooted in historical and systemic injustices, such as slavery, segregation, colonialism, and institutional racism, which continue to shape social and economic outcomes for generations.

Economic inequality, for example, is driven by disparities in income and wealth distribution, with the wealthiest individuals and corporations accumulating disproportionate power and resources while millions of Americans struggle to make ends meet and achieve economic security. Racial discrimination and inequality persist in areas such as employment, education, healthcare, and criminal justice, with communities of color facing systemic barriers and biases that limit opportunities and perpetuate cycles of poverty and marginalization.

Addressing Social Injustice and Inequality:

Addressing social injustice and inequality requires a comprehensive and multi-faceted approach that addresses the root causes of disparities and promotes equity, inclusion, and justice in all aspects of society. This includes efforts to dismantle systemic racism and discrimination, promote economic opportunity and mobility, ensure access to essential services and rights, and empower marginalized communities to advocate for their rights and interests.

Dismantling Systemic Racism and Discrimination:

Systemic racism and discrimination are entrenched in American society, perpetuating inequalities and injustices that disproportionately affect communities of color. To dismantle systemic racism and discrimination, it is essential to confront biases and prejudices, reform discriminatory policies and practices, and promote racial equity and justice in all aspects of society.

This may include initiatives such as criminal justice reform to address racial disparities in policing, sentencing, and incarceration, educational equity initiatives to promote access to quality education and eliminate disparities in school funding and resources, and economic empowerment programs to address disparities in employment, wages, and wealth accumulation.

Additionally, efforts to promote diversity, equity, and inclusion in workplaces, institutions, and communities are essential for creating environments that value and celebrate difference and ensure that all individuals have the opportunity to thrive and succeed regardless of their race, ethnicity, or background.

Promoting Economic Opportunity and Mobility:

Economic inequality is a major driver of social injustice and inequality, limiting opportunities and perpetuating cycles of poverty and marginalization for millions of Americans. To promote economic opportunity and mobility, it is essential to address disparities in income, wealth, and access to economic resources and opportunities.

This may include initiatives such as raising the minimum wage, implementing progressive tax policies to redistribute wealth and resources, and investing in education, job training, and workforce development programs to equip individuals with the skills and opportunities they need to succeed in the 21st-century economy.

Additionally, efforts to promote affordable housing, healthcare, childcare, and other essential services are essential for ensuring that all individuals and families have access to the resources and support they need to thrive and achieve economic security.

Ensuring Access to Essential Services and Rights:

Access to essential services and rights, such as healthcare, education, housing, and voting, is essential for promoting social justice and equity and ensuring that all individuals have the opportunity to lead healthy, dignified, and fulfilling lives.

To ensure access to essential services and rights, it is essential to eliminate barriers and disparities that limit opportunities and perpetuate inequalities for marginalized communities. This may include initiatives such as expanding access to affordable healthcare through initiatives such as Medicaid expansion and the Affordable Care Act, investing in public education and school desegregation efforts to ensure equitable access to quality education for all students, and implementing policies to promote affordable housing and combat housing discrimination.

Additionally, efforts to protect and expand voting rights, civil rights, and human rights are essential for ensuring that all individuals have a voice in shaping the policies and decisions that affect their lives and communities.

Empowering Marginalized Communities:

Empowering marginalized communities to advocate for their rights and interests is essential for fostering social justice and equity and building a more inclusive and just society. This may include initiatives such as community organizing and activism, civic engagement and leadership development programs, and initiatives to amplify the voices and experiences of marginalized communities in policymaking and decision-making processes.

Additionally, efforts to address disparities in political representation and participation, such as voter suppression and gerrymandering, are essential for ensuring that all individuals have equal access to the political process and can advocate for their rights and interests.

Conclusion:

Fostering social justice and equity is essential for building a more inclusive, equitable, and just society where all individuals have the opportunity to thrive and succeed regardless of their race, ethnicity, gender, or socioeconomic status. By addressing systemic injustices and disparities, promoting economic opportunity and mobility, ensuring access to essential services and rights, and empowering marginalized communities to advocate for their rights and interests, we can create a future where social justice and equity are at the forefront of decision-making and where all individuals and communities have the opportunity to live with dignity, respect, and equality. However, achieving meaningful progress on social justice and equity will require political will, collective action, and a commitment to upholding the rights and dignity of all individuals and communities. With bold action and a shared vision, we can build a future where social justice and equity are the foundation of a more just and equitable world for generations to come.